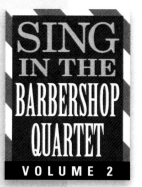

SING IN THE BARBERSHOP QUARTET VOLUME 2

ROCK IN HARMONY

CONTENTS

PLAYBACK+
Speed • Pitch • Balance • Loop

To access audio, visit:
www.halleonard.com/mylibrary

Enter Code
2846-9197-8793-3427

Beginning pitches on the audio are the root (tonic) of the song's key.

ISBN 978-1-4234-6180-7

HAL•LEONARD®
7777 W. BLUEMOUND RD. P.O. BOX 13819 MILWAUKEE, WI 53213

Visit Hal Leonard Online at
www.halleonard.com

The Banana Boat Song

**Arrangement by
DON GRAY**

**Lyric and Music by ERIK DARLING,
BOB CAREY and ALAN ARKIN**

* Measures 1-2 and 5-6 may be sung by leads only or a soloist.

4

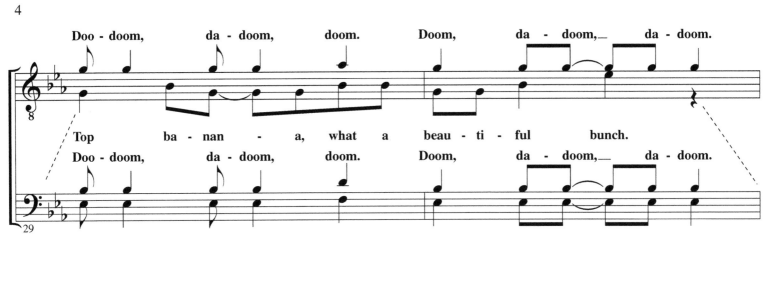

Measures 33-34 and 37-38 may be sung by leads only or a soloist.

Hello Mary Lou

Arrangement by
DAVID WRIGHT

Words and Music by GENE PITNEY
and C. MANGIARACINA

6

Verse 2

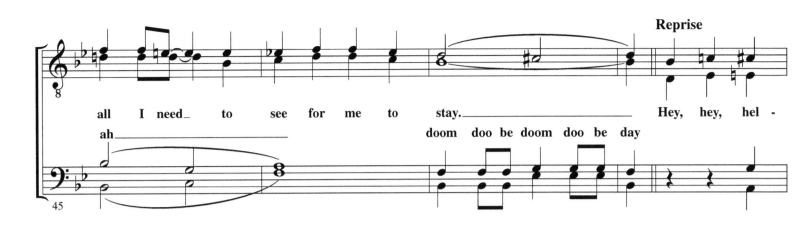

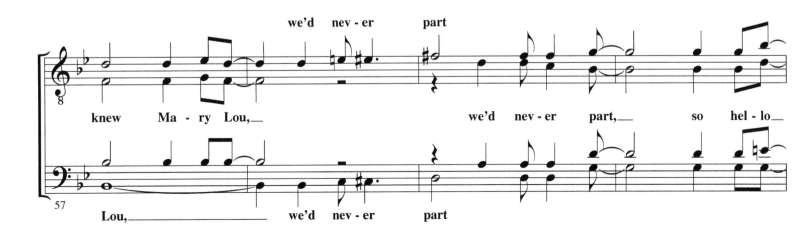

Goodnight, Sweetheart, Goodnight
(Goodnight, It's Time to Go)

**Arrangement by
MEL KNIGHT**

**Words and Music by JAMES HUDSON
and CALVIN CARTER**

15

Happy Together

Arrangement by
LIZ GARNETT

Words and Music by GARRY BONNER
and ALAN GORDON

doot　doot　doot　doot　doot　doot　doot　doot

call　you　up,　　in - vest　a　dime,　　and　you　say　you　be -

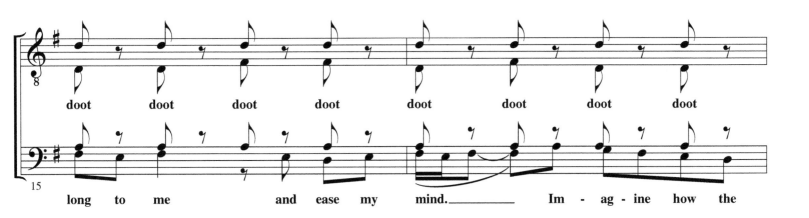

doot　doot　doot　doot　doot　doot　doot　doot

long　to　me　　and　ease　my　mind.＿＿＿　Im - ag - ine　how　the

doot　doot　doot　doot　fine,　so　hap - py　to - geth - er,　to -

world　could　be,　　so　ver - y　fine,　so　hap - py　to - geth - er.＿＿＿

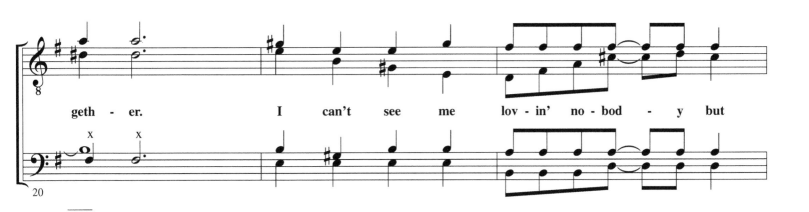

geth - er.　　I　can't　see　me　lov - in'　no - bod - y　but

ba ba da

you for all my life._____ When you're with me,

ba ba da

for

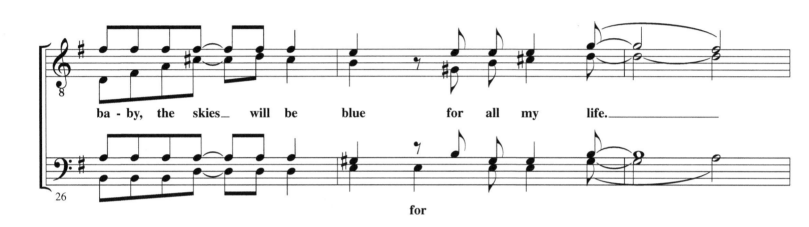

ba - by, the skies__ will be blue for all my life._____

for

Doot doot doot doot doot doot doot doot

Doot me an' you doot you an' me doot doot

Me an' you, and you an' me, no mat - ter how they

doot doot doot doot doot doot doot doot

doot toss the dice doot doot doot on - ly one for

toss the dice, it had to be._____ The on - ly one for

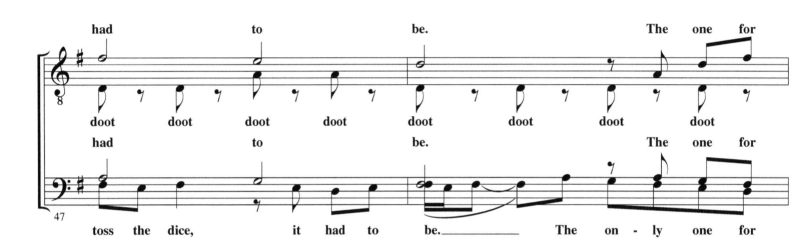

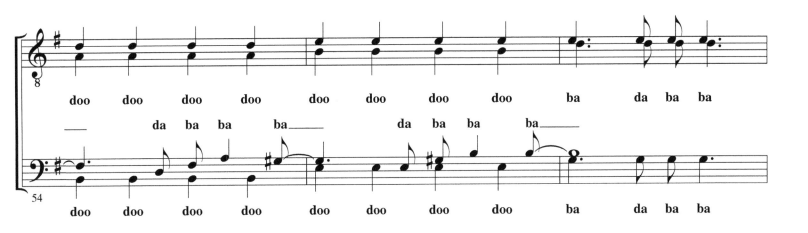

doo doo doo doo doo doo doo doo ba da ba ba
da ba ba ba____ da ba ba ba____
doo doo doo doo doo doo doo doo ba da ba ba

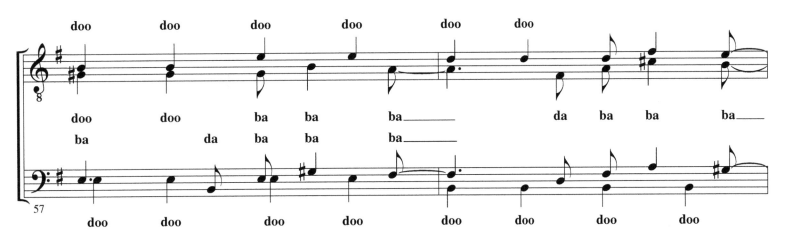

doo doo doo doo doo doo
doo doo ba ba ba____ da ba ba ba____
ba da ba ba ba____
doo doo doo doo doo doo doo doo

da ba ba ba____ da ba ba____
doo doo doo doo doo da ba ba____

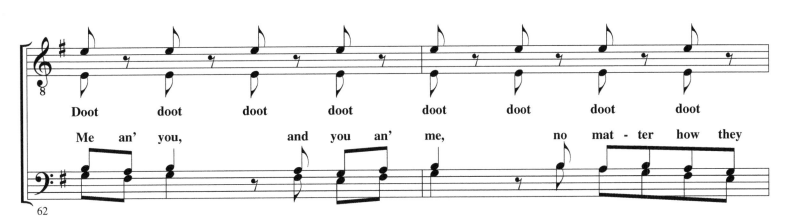

Doot doot doot doot doot doot doot doot
Me an' you, and you an' me, no mat- ter how they

22

In My Room

Arrangement by
TOM GENTRY

Words and Music by BRIAN WILSON
and GARY USHER

* Lead (or other voice part) delivers a spoken introduction to set the mood of the song.

The Longest Time

**Arrangement by
TOM GENTRY**

Words and Music by
BILLY JOEL

28

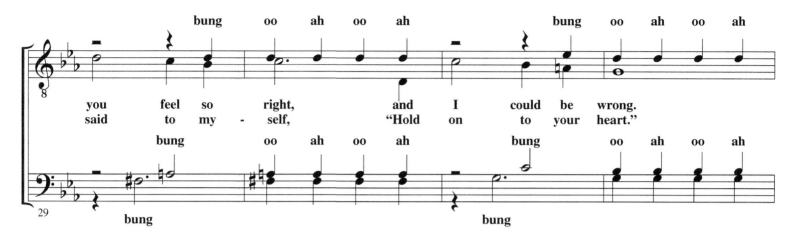

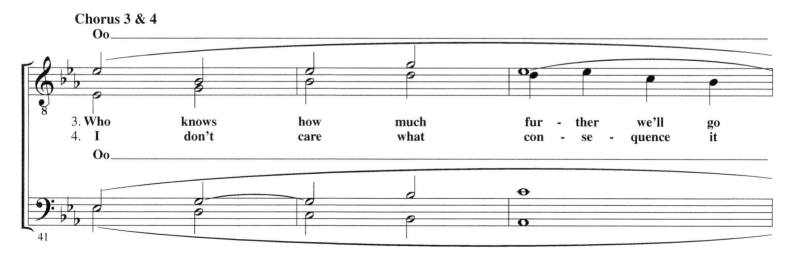

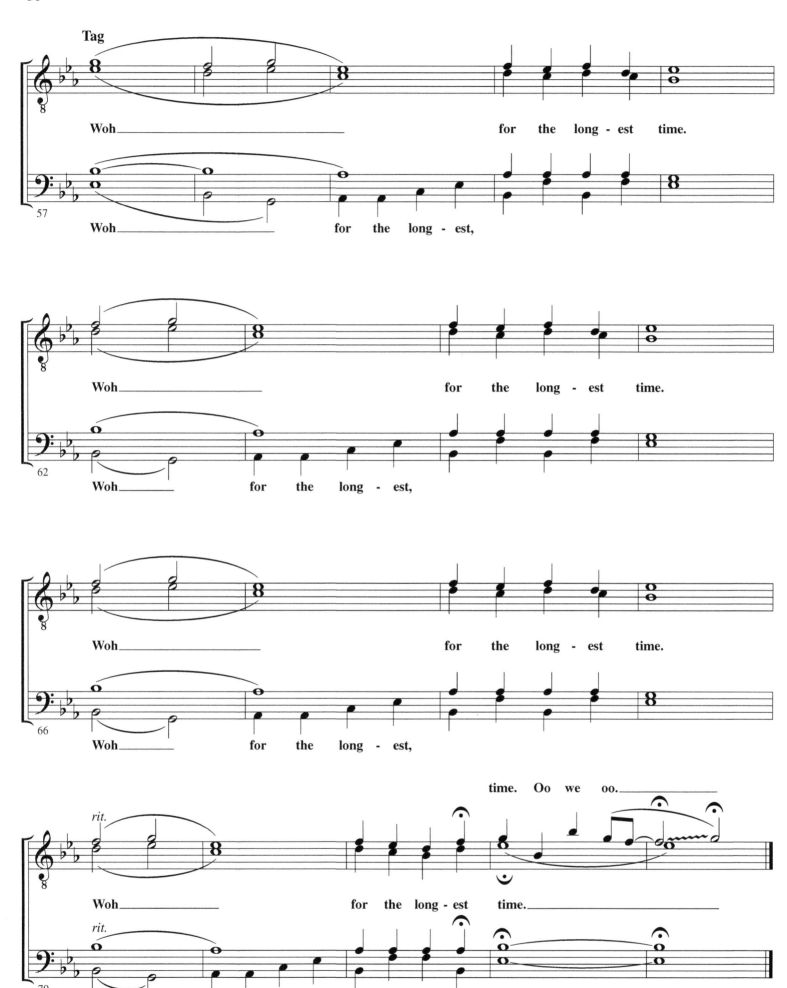

Silhouettes

Arrangement by
TOM GENTRY

Words and Music by FRANK C. SLAY JR.
and BOB CREWE

34

Under the Boardwalk

Arrangement by
SPEBSQSA, INC.

Words and Music by ARTIE RESNICK
and KENNY YOUNG

38